T0381190

VS

Vital Signs

POETRY • PROSE • LIFE SCENES

BY JOHN LAWRENCE BARBETTA

WITH, J.H. WOLF & G.T. MAKOUSKY

AuthorHouse™
1663 Liberty Drive
Bloomington, IN 47403
www.authorhouse.com
Phone: 1 (800) 839-8640

Published by AuthorHouse 11/18/2015

ISBN: 978-1-5049-5512-6 (sc)
ISBN: 978-1-5049-5513-3 (e)

Library of Congress Control Number: 2015916875

Print information available on the last page.

Any people depicted in stock imagery provided by Thinkstock are models,
and such images are being used for illustrative purposes only.
Certain stock imagery © Thinkstock.

This book is printed on acid-free paper.

Because of the dynamic nature of the Internet, any web addresses or links contained in this book may have changed
since publication and may no longer be valid. The views expressed in this work are solely those of the author and do not
necessarily reflect the views of the publisher, and the publisher hereby disclaims any responsibility for them.

author**HOUSE**®

My life as child, boy, man. My life as father, teacher, poet. Seems to have one common, tenuous thread. I have always sought after beauty. An innocent quest to discover something, someone that radiated a quality that I would finally recognize as beauty. When five I pinched tiny wild violets growing in the cracks of the city sidewalks. "Fiori di leprechauns", flowers of the leprechauns they became known in my Italian- Irish neighborhood. As I grew older my journey took me from suburb, to farm country. The adventure included New York, Boston, Maine, Minnesota, Wisconsin, Portugal, TheNetherlands. All hold inspired memories from which I draw creative energy. All were and are the homes of family and friends who feed my spirit, nourish my soul. To all who have loved me, cared for me, think kindly of me, I dedicate this work, as I have dedicated my life to you. In you I have discovered the ever elusive Beauty.

On Beauty

(heart vision)

Not in the eye of the beholder
To see it you need vision bolder
Not the sum of the parts,
The connection of hearts
Enables the appearance of beauty.
Beauty is shy
It hides from aggression
The more desperate the search
The more elusive possession
It is quick silver to touch
too little, too much
A glint and then gone
The sunset or dawn
Did you see it or not?
Real or a dream?
The soul's endless quest
escapes conscious scheme.
No binder or frame can contain
no human recall
Divinely perceived or
not seen at all.

Uncommon Senses

My eyes sip the lemon sea
I inhale its salty spice
and the sugar sweet bouquet of wild roses
I taste the juicy sunset orange
and the mist of farewell tears chills my heart
I touch the silk purple coverlet clouds
and smooth them over restive waves
I listen to the pulse of the cold blue star
and sing a silent song of longing
I reach up to embrace the gathering truth
I kiss the unabashed face of mother moon
I know the cause of every wrinkle.
I fall into a sated state
Dream and yet awakened
I have a sense of time and self and place
I need only to savor the manna of nature
To sustain my spiritual life.

Ask yourself.

Why glower, when you can glow?
Why gloat, when you can smile?
Why look, when you can see?
Why listen, when you can hear?
Why touch, when you can feel?
Why gulp, when you can savor?
Why build a wall, when you can build a bridge?
Why judge, when you can embrace?
Why hate, when you can love?
Why exist, when you can live?

On my virtual US tour with Pope Francis (Papa Francisco) September 22-27, 2015

these are some life choices that came to mind.

Mutual respect. Reverence for life. Peace.

just me

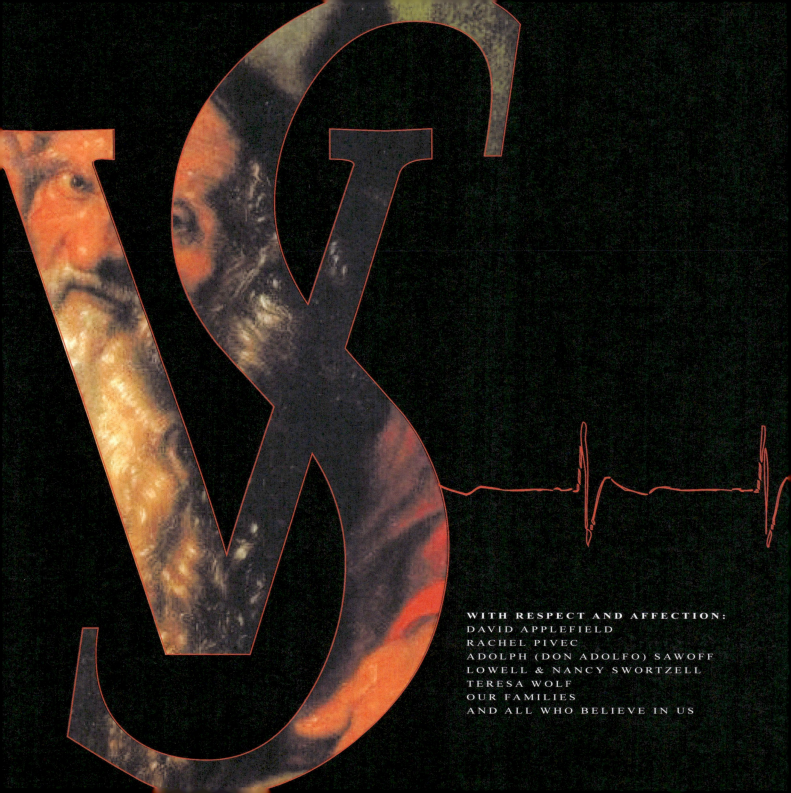

WITH RESPECT AND AFFECTION:
DAVID APPLEFIELD
RACHEL PIVEC
ADOLPH (DON ADOLFO) SAWOFF
LOWELL & NANCY SWORTZELL
TERESA WOLF
OUR FAMILIES
AND ALL WHO BELIEVE IN US

"unOpened"

I closed my eyes
that I may see
I blocked out sound
that I may hear
I erased memory
that I may feel
I sealed lips
that I may speak
I opened my heart
that I may imagine.....

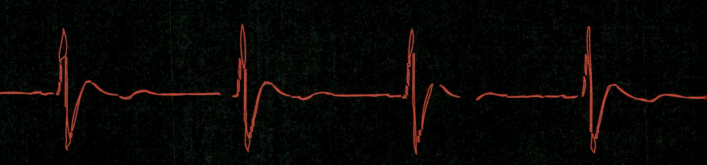

WORDS : **John Lawrence Barbetta**
IMAGE : **John Howard Wolf**
DESIGN : **Geoffrey Makousky**

"LIGHT"

Light is the source of
inspiration and revelation.
It provides a flicker glimpse
of profound truth.
What greater gift than light?
Not the ability to approve
it on canvas or paper,
but simply to be an attentive
witness as to its wonder.
I am such a witness.

When we were young, we were more pretty.
Now, we are old and more beautiful.

ARE
UTIFUL

chapter **1**:unSeen

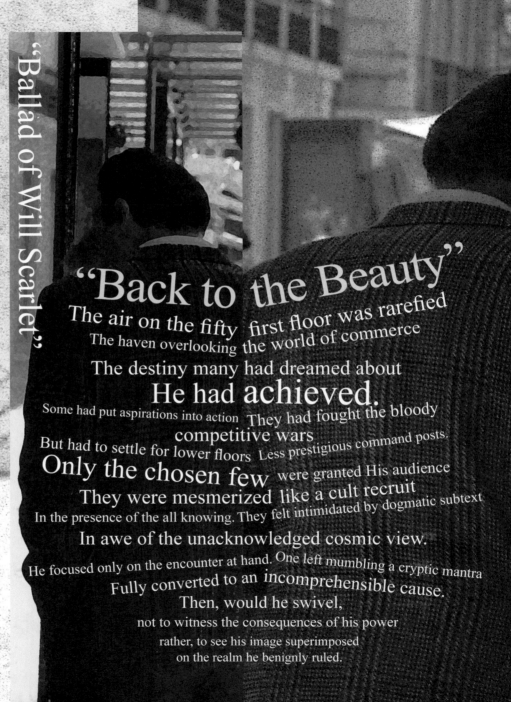

"Ballad of Will Scarlet"

He lay on the concrete
Hand in the gutter
Blood trickled down drain
He could hear people mutter
He's just a kid
A guy from the hood
I heard he did drugs
He was up to no good
From a crack in the walk
Came the aura of life
He pinched a nosegay
Kiss goodbye his street wife
No Robin or Maid
to share his last song
Scarlet breath scattered seeds
Some lodged in hope fractures
Will they bring
flowers or weeds?

"Back to the Beauty"

The air on the fifty first floor was rarefied
The haven overlooking the world of commerce
The destiny many had dreamed about
He had **achieved.**
Some had put aspirations into action They had fought the bloody
competitive wars
But had to settle for lower floors Less prestigious command posts.
Only the chosen few were granted His audience
They were mesmerized like a cult recruit
In the presence of the all knowing. They felt intimidated by dogmatic subtext
In awe of the unacknowledged cosmic view.
He focused only on the encounter at hand. One left mumbling a cryptic mantra
Fully converted to an incomprehensible cause.
Then, would he swivel,
not to witness the consequences of his power
rather, to see his image superimposed
on the realm he benignly ruled.

"American Dream"

The child slept on the unforgiving concrete walk
An aura of contentment made radiant the hustle bustle dirt and dust.

What could she possibly be dreaming?

The sounds of cars whisk her away to a safer, softer place of trees and grasses.

The smell of food from the clattering restaurant
becomes a source of strength flavored with the love for which she hungers.

People voice annoyance or amusement
That she blocks their way. Suddenly, they stop,
scoop her up and in protective arms carry her to the warm, whisper-world, Home.

There she clutches security, comfort.
She smells and tastes. Respect nourishing body and spirit.
She hears healing sounds of concern, hope, affection.
This is where she belongs. This is her rightful destiny. This is Home.

Oh, that such deserving Sweet Street Dreams come true.

How are you?
I hope you're doing better than me.

I had a little set back.
I lost my job. My wife is leaving me.
I'm drinking, again.

It's only temporary.
I have no idea what to do next.

I don't mean to bother you with this stuff.
You're the only person on the planet who gives a damn.

I'll call you, when I figure things out.
Probably, collect from Mexico.

Thanks for your card.
The snowmen celebrating the New Year reminded me of us.
I'm heading out for the local.
I'll have one for you.

If you get a chance…
For Christ's sake come over.

How about those Vikings?!
Who the f… cares?

Merry Christmas to you and the family.
You lucky bastard.

Later. Jimmy

Holiday he-Mail

Some of my best friends are flowers.
Some of the people I most admire are weeds.

"Our gift

is new eyes

with which

to see

the familiar"

I donated my poetry to charity, they shredded it.
Reason? It wasn't hard bound.

"FOOL"

I wonder, with no apologies or regrets,
why when I polish a glass,
do I expect a genie to appear?
Why do I give drink to a plant with no blossom of life?
Why do I look for a flower
a month before the spring thaw?
Why do I believe in peace and in people,
when war and killing are the realities du jour?
Because I am a fool.
Because I am a blissful, unrepentant fool.

chapter2:unHeard

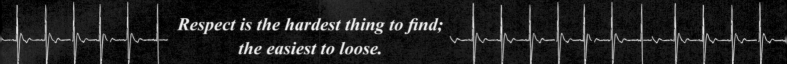

I found it in a trash can
near the Granada movie theater

I was throwing away a box of candy
(Not Good, though there was Plenty)

Who in the world would throw an old **sax** away?

"Jazz Santa"

I remembered a black man that use to play

Jazz music on a nearby corner

Some wise guys must have taken it.

I followed a melody in my head

to the place I remembered

There he sat

on a

peeling

wood

bar

stool

He played on a brand new instrument

The street light came on as I approached

He wore a green hat, red scarf

fingerless red gloves

Snow started to fall

He

"You can keep it."

stopped

"Merry Christmas."

playing.

It was.

A stranger is a friend

"Screams"

I saw the flower weep
No butterfly came to call.
The tree moaned
Wind tore leaves
from pleading branches.
Grasslands drowned
by drunken waters
I witnessed the sweet
sand washed bitter
by greedy sea
Innocent sun swallowed
by the suffocating clouds
I heard the air choking
on indifference
I heard my neighbor scream:
"I need dignity!"
I echo the scream
for the mournful flower,
grasslands and tree
Voiceless beach, life giving sun
Unheard neighbors, and, yes, me
Scream! Scream!
"WE ALL NEED DIGNITY"!

I wish to free all the Sibyls from their cages
I wish to vanquish all the pain suffered through the ages.

"Time Flits"

Time does not fly.
Sometimes it skips along
carefree a wordless song
Then, you fall
bruise your heart.
A kiss of hope
A new, scar tissue start.
In dreams you fly
In life you try
to leave petty thoughts behind
elevate above the dead, the dying
Reach a place only you can find
No map to guide you
Close your eyes
Stand barefoot in imagined sand.
Time flits.
You are flying.

"Free Voice"

I could not make it rhyme
I could not keep the rhythm
The meter did not matter
My soul urged me to shout
That someone else may hear me
That some other soul might care
Was there someone
Anyone out there?
My message was pain muddled
My need was life intense
Please, please acknowledge
I am here
and that I matter
to any one somewhere.
"Hello, anybody!
Is any one out there?"

"I banged

my head

until the

words

fell out."

"POETS"

It is said, "poets are the least liars
" I have always aspired to be a member
of this life affirming society.
Poetry is the distillation of human feelings.
The images that inspire us to the realization that:
"Love is a verb."
Its only utility is when we release
its potential through humane acts.

I am not older than you.
I have lived longer

chapter3:unSpoken

Until

I wish to stare
at the clouds
Until I can see
what they hide.
I want to gaze
at the stars
Until I perceive
the lessons they light.
I want to glare
at the sun
Until it melts
truth from self-pride.
I want to listen
to the birds
Until I remember
the words of their song.
I wish to dance
with the leaves
Until rhythm is pulse
I want to kiss
the fickle wind
Until there is
one shared breath.

"I can't write in the
RAIN."

*"Then, get an umbrella
and a spray for the mold.
Get on with your writing
your excuses are old:
No time
No inspiration
No space.*

*Make time
Find Inspiration
Make space."*

Tears of the angels
Swell buds into blossoms
Hope bubbles from earth
Hearts ride on the waves
I glide to my haven
Thoughts now flow free
It is doubt
Not the rain
Fear of risk
Not the pain

"I can, I will write in the rain."

"Words,

words,

words."

Looking for the words
Searching to express the feeling
Praying to communicate
The strain
The pain
The pleasure
The value of the treasure
The happiness
I can't express
Not in words or phrases
simple or complex.
Perhaps, in deeds.
Embrace
A kiss
A whispered sound
consent of understanding.
The dam that shields
the arid heart is pierced
by instinct, impulse
The eloquence of subtext.

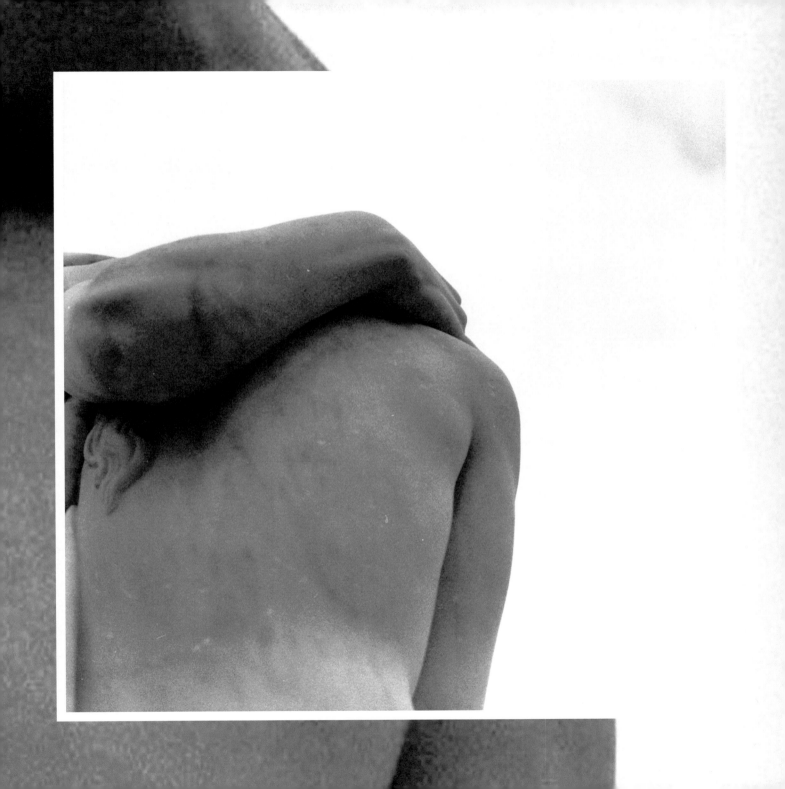

Orpheus, they have cut you limb from limb.
Yet to their dismay, you sing and sing.

"To be

inspired

is good fortune.

To be

inspiring

is dedication."

"GIFT"

*Compassion is nature's energy
to break walls of time and place
Yes, end mortality.
Time together is our reparation
In life and death no separation.
Our children are our legacy
Love's gift our immortality.*

chapter4:unFelt

"Fingerprint"

There's a fingerprint on my face.
I wonder who put it there?
It does seem a bit out of place
I've noted that some people stare
Not the mark of affection
It's an inky collection
A warning reflection.
The one who did it meant harm
Poke at my cheek
Under the eye
Mean spirit sneak
It stings when I cry.
Not tears for lost perfection
The cause is mournful recollection
Ill willed genetic selection.
I'm afraid..who did it meant harm.
There's a fingerprint on my face
I think I know who put it there.

"Hide & Seek"

Today the pillow
stuck to my head
The sheets were my skin
The mattress my twin
My body the bed.
The song of the bird
a dissonant shriek
pine furniture moan
a deafening creak
I clamped my mouth shut
I explode if I speak.
I hid glasses from sight
that my vision stay hazy
The light through filter
Shaded thoughts
undefined, soft and lazy
Flowers were rude
Beauty seemed crude.
I'm craving for silence
escape from the dun
A moment alone
Endless embrace of the sun.

"Pleasure of Pain"

It hurts when I walk
when I try to rise or sit.
The pain I feel
is sometimes fire-like.
Sometimes a stab
or blow below the belt.
Then, there is the constant irritation
eye or groin or abdomen.
The angst created by
mirrored reminders
of scars and bruising.

The positive?

I can still feel a concerned touch
Read an encouraging note
Taste a favorite food
Listen to caring voices
Dream of sweeter yesterdays
Kinder tomorrows
Hope for nature's cure or relief
Pray for those who
suffer far worse pain
and have far less solace.
I can still feel.

"Sweet Company"

The wind shouted obscenities
The tree shook and bent
She clutched delicate,
innocent blossoms.
The merciless wind prevailed
The tree stood humiliated
Distraught, despondent
Denied its destiny.
In the quiet after the storm,
a healing sound diminished the pain
She raised her naked branches as in prayer
Anticipating a gentle miracle
like the soft rains that urged her to grow
despite burning sun, times of blight
human neglect.
From the hopeful sky came the source of song
Landing lightly on her welcoming limbs
Simple brown, as the earth from which she sprang,
an amorous partner sang and sang and sang
Until the brutal encounter, life stealing energy
seemed a reconcilable memory.
The winged messenger appeared with the sun
He would make music, she would dance
Sweet balance -Inspiration.

Faithful reunions continued
Her unfailing companion
became her loquacious lover.
One day of fearful premonition
harsh wind returned
Wind's shouts sucked the life sap
from all who felt its dragon breath.
Tree stood tall, defiant
Anchored by deepening roots
Pride conquered submission.
Repelled force whirled about,
Sister willows waved a sardonic farewell;
Tears of joy came from the heavens.

Do not rest until you have made
that glint of light the sun.

"HOPE"

I have tried to instill and keep hope alive
in the hearts of those with whom
I have shared time and thought.
I followed my impulse to reinforce
dignity and a sense of self worth.
Can I evoke a smile,
or better yet, a laugh,
from those whose spirits
are in the shadows?
Can I induce a glimmer
of life affirming joy
that tomorrow could be,
will be, a better day.
Sometimes I have been successful;
other times not.
I do know I will continue to try.

"If you can't speak. Sing.

If you can't walk. Dance."

chapter5:unImagined

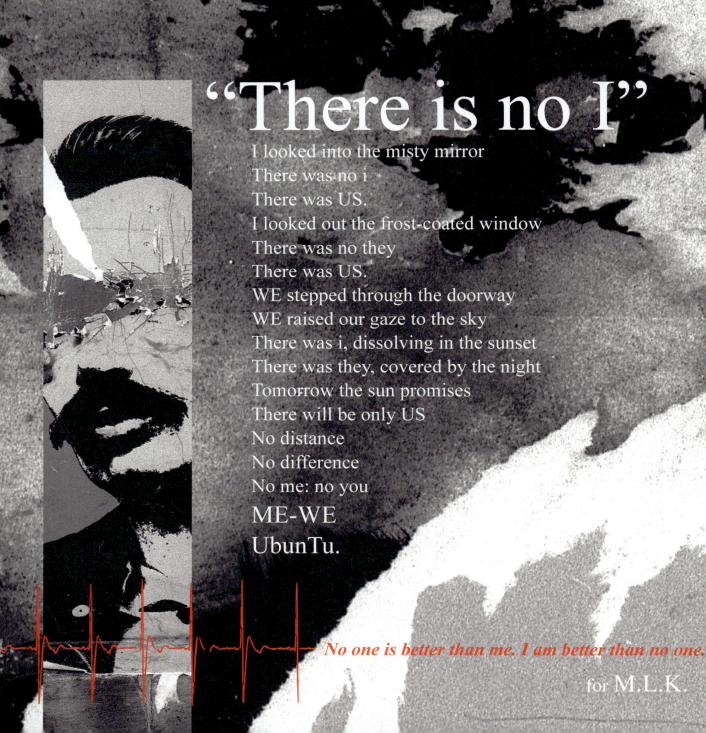

"There is no I"

I looked into the misty mirror
There was no i
There was US.
I looked out the frost-coated window
There was no they
There was US.
WE stepped through the doorway
WE raised our gaze to the sky
There was i, dissolving in the sunset
There was they, covered by the night
Tomorrow the sun promises
There will be only US
No distance
No difference
No me: no you
ME-WE
UbunTu.

No one is better than me. I am better than no one.

for M.L.K.

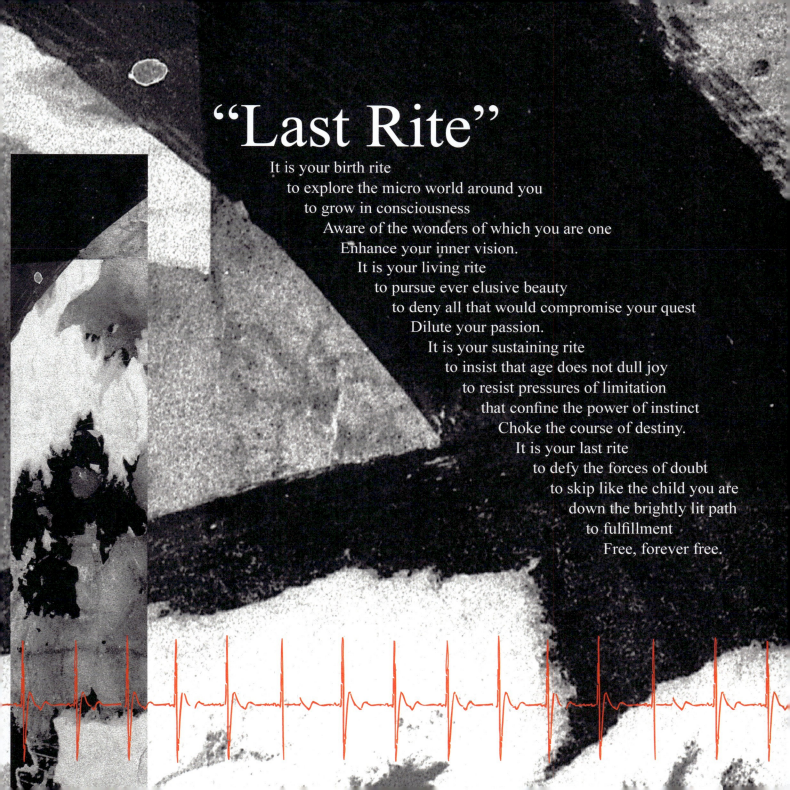

"Last Rite"

It is your birth rite
to explore the micro world around you
to grow in consciousness
Aware of the wonders of which you are one
Enhance your inner vision.
It is your living rite
to pursue ever elusive beauty
to deny all that would compromise your quest
Dilute your passion.
It is your sustaining rite
to insist that age does not dull joy
to resist pressures of limitation
that confine the power of instinct
Choke the course of destiny.
It is your last rite
to defy the forces of doubt
to skip like the child you are
down the brightly lit path
to fulfillment
Free, forever free.

It lay discarded
on the terrace tiles
a thin, inconsequential
wood stick with **blackened** tip
A bit of trash   Ignored or swept away

Appeared *to be its destiny*

No reward or consideration
for the *inspiring* light
created for soul locked *lovers*

the comfort and *warmth of reunion*

it had sparked
the *despair* of darkness
it had **banished**.

There it lay

Utility, function finished
a thankless journey

from tree chip to ash.
Its legacy?

Unrequited enlightenment.

"Matchstick Man"

"Out of Touch"
(Doubting Thomas)

I am full of doubt.
I touch your wound
Does my doubt
make it deeper?
I feel your pain
Is it eased that I share it?

I want to believe
There is hope
Goodness lives
That I am worthy
Forsaken forgives.

Please touch my wound
Heal consternation
Let blood blend with blood
No separation
No doubt
No confusion
Mutual faith
God- human fusion.

Humankind will believe what they see.
And believe in what they cannot see.

In Praise of Folly

(I think. Therefore, I act.)

I feel the cold shell
that housed the insights
that gives direction
to me and those yet to come.

I read your thoughts
The heart and mind struggle
to reach the destination of truth.

Truth as we mortals
can imperfectly conceive it.

Like a sacred conch
held to my soul
I can hear the crashing
waterfall of human concern
that corruption and hypocrisy
have poisoned once holy waters.

Reason is being drowned
by the torrent of
righteous rational-lies.

As long as I breathe
I shall perpetuate your legacy
of truth, and reason.
I dedicate my life-time energy
to thoughtful observation
Love inspired action.

Rational-lies are like a sponge soaked in vinegar
offered to the thirsty.

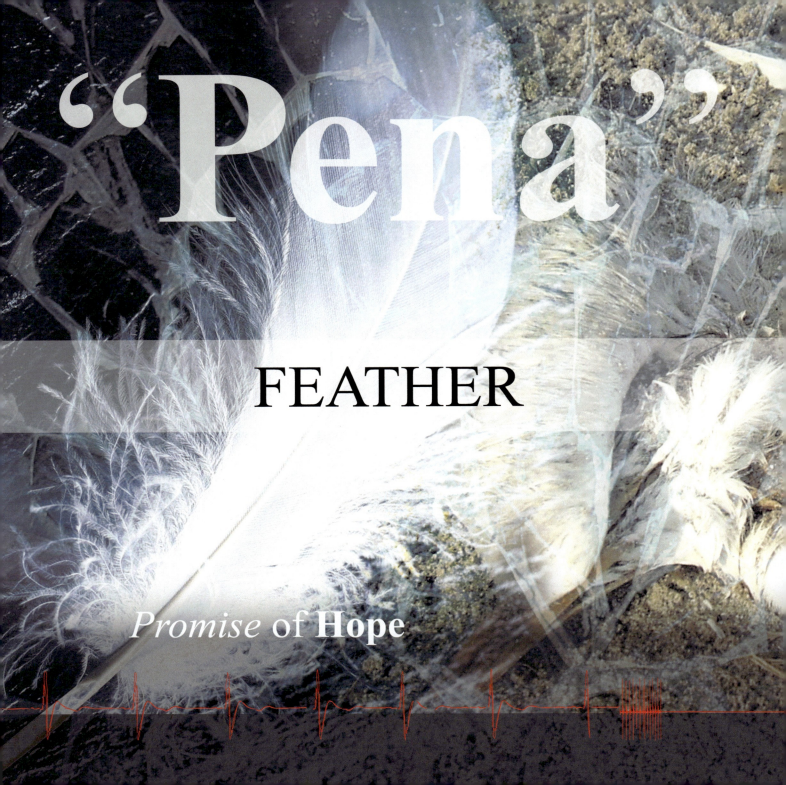

PITY

PEN

Denial of **Hope**

Renewal of **Hope**

GOD IS IN THE DETAILS

"Don't part with your *illusions*.
When they are gone you may still exist,
but you have ceased to *live*."

Mark Twain

Parting

Could you stay a little longer?
It's been such a lovely visit
I don't know where the time has gone
Laughter makes the hours fly
Tears and pain I can't recall
The pleasure of your company
helped me rise above it all.

You warmed me in the winter
with words that promised Spring
You kept every single promise
You ever made to me
How I wish I could freeze frame time
Forever we would be
A living portrait of mirrored souls
Defying change and convention
Eternally preserved in a place unspoiled,
a timeless context created by shared wonder
A never ending day of welcome mist
No fear of goodbye thunder.

Printed in the United States
By Bookmasters